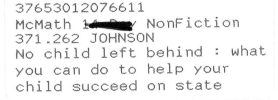

Test Prep and Admissions

No Child Left Behind:

What You Can Do to Help Your Child Succeed on State Tests

Cynthia and Drew Johnson

Simon & Schuster

NEW YORK · LONDON · SYDNEY · TORONTO

Kaplan Publishing
Published by SIMON & SCHUSTER
Rockefeller Center
1230 Avenue of the Americas
New York, NY 10020

All of the practice questions in this book were created by the authors to illustrate question
types. They are not actual test questions.

Contributing Editor: Seppy Basili
Editorial Director: Jennifer Farthing
Project Editor: Eileen McDonnell
Editorial Assistant: Nina Monti
Production Manager: Michael Shevlin
Cover Design: Mark Weaver

Manufactured in the United States of America.
Published simultaneously in Canada.

10 9 8 7 6 5 4 3 2 1

September 2005

ISBN-13: 978-0-7432-5187-7
ISBN-10:   0-7432-5187-3

For information regarding special discounts for bulk purchases,
please contact Simon & Schuster Special Sales at 1-800-456-6798 or
business@simonandschuster.com.

CONTENTS

Acknowledgments   vii

Introduction   ix

Chapter One: The A's, B's, C's, and D's of Good Test Taking   1

Chapter Two: Reading Skills   15

Chapter Three: Writing Section   29

Chapter Four: How the Math Test Adds Up   33

Chapter Five: I Got a What?!   49

List of State Exams, Grades 3–5   53

List of State Test Websites   59

Glossary   63

Acknowledgments

The authors would like to thank Maureen McMahon, Lori DeGeorge, and Charli Engelhorn for their enormous contributions towards making this book a reality.

INTRODUCTION

Education in America is constantly changing. Twenty-five years ago, only a small number of schools had a computer anywhere in the building. Now, entire schools are connected by a network of machines in every room. School uniforms were in fashion, then they weren't, and now they are coming back. Of course, not everything has changed. School lunches are still school lunches, P.E. class is still P.E. class, and tests are still tests. Only now there are more tests.

There have always been classroom tests, such as pop quizzes, chapter reviews, and final exams. However, starting in the 1990s, many states began requiring students to take comprehensive, annual standardized tests. These exams were designed to ensure that the typical student learned the basic math and reading skills for their grade. In many states, a failing grade on these exams meant that the student had to take summer school, repeat the grade, and/or retake the test until earning a passing grade. The overall goal of these annual tests was to add a level of accountability to the American educational system, and this accountability was not simply for the students. Teachers were judged on how well their students performed. Entire schools were placed on academic probation if their test scores remained too low and showed no improvement over a period of time. Superintendents were replaced at low-scoring districts.

The growth of these *high-stakes* exams signaled a new trend in America's educational system. Many educators and politicians believed these tests would give states a chance to identify at-risk students and get them the extra help they needed, instead of just moving them through the system. To help ensure the success of these exams, the No Child Left Behind Act was passed in 2002. This act mandated that by 2005, every state must give an annual math test and reading test to all students in grades 3–8. Find more information about the No Child Left Behind Act at http://www.ed.gov/nclb.

Fifty States Equals Fifty Different Tests, Right?
Not Exactly....

The No Child Left Behind Act requires each state to give students math and reading tests, but the law does not say exactly *which* test must be used. This means that the state of Florida can still use its version of a standardized test (known as the Florida Comprehensive Assessment Test), while Illinois continues to use its own test (Illinois Standards Achievement Test). This is good news for those states because scrapping one test and implementing another would cost a great deal of time and money.

There are now 50 states using 50 different exams. If each test was truly unique, it would be difficult, if not impossible, to write a book like the one you are holding in your hands. There would just be too many differences from one state to the next.

However, the tests are not that different from each other. Consider that all of these tests are designed to see whether or not students have learned the basic math and reading skills for their grade level. There is little disagreement about what constitutes basic grade school math and reading skills. Some states might use the phrase *spatial figures* instead of *geometry*, but they are still talking about triangles, circles, and squares. In other words:

The basic math and reading skills are the same for all states. Each state's standardized test is designed to test whether or not students have learned these skills. Because the basic skills are so similar, most state tests are also similar.

This holds true for national standardized tests as well. Large national tests like the Stanford, Terra Nova, and Iowa Test of Basic Skills (ITBS) vary somewhat in format and structure, but they are still focused on the same basic math and reading skills. This means that many test sections are similar in structure and content. None of the tests are exactly alike: The point is that most of the tests share a great deal of similarity.

Therefore, if Greg Pupil learns some basic math and reading test strategies, Greg should be able to apply those strategies successfully on a wide variety of tests. These strategies should help him on his annual state exam, regardless of what state he lives in. These same strategies will also help him on any major national standardized test because these have a lot in common with many state tests.

We have written this guide to describe these basic math and reading test-taking strategies. Our goal is to provide you with the basic information needed to help you prepare your children for most state standardized math and reading tests. In addition to math and reading strategies, there are also some general test-taking strategies that are useful on most standardized tests. Granted, every test has its quirks, so this book is not going to prepare your child for every question on every test; no book could. Even so, there are many common question types, and this book will provide you with the useful strategies for answering these questions.

How to Use This Book

Every strong building needs a good foundation. Think of this book as the foundation for a good approach to test taking. A child who learns the strategies included here will be able to tackle most basic standardized tests.

Most states agree on the general information that their grade school students are required to learn, but there is often some minor variation in which grade level it is first taught. Consider the concept of geometry. One state might start with simple perimeter questions in the third grade and move to harder questions concerning a figure's area by the fifth grade. Another state might organize it differently starting with simple figures—like a square—in the third grade and then move on to tougher figures in the fifth grade. These different approaches could subtly affect the material your child learns in the third, fourth, and fifth grades. However, in the end, it is all still geometry, and the same basic knowledge is required.

This book is designed to cover the basic concepts associated with grades 3–5. Whenever applicable, we will note when a concept is harder (more likely to appear in the fifth grade) or easier (more likely to appear in the third grade). But keep in mind that these designations will be influenced by the state you are living in.

The material in this book is up-to-date at the time of publication. For more information on standardized tests in your state, visit the state department of education's website listed at the back of the book.

Chapter One   THE A's, B's, C's, AND D's OF GOOD TEST TAKING

Understanding a Test is Half the Battle

Does the mere sight of a No. 2 pencil cause your child to break into a cold, trembling sweat? Are the words *multiple choice* or *essay* invariably followed by a thin, keening shriek or forlorn wail? If the answer to either of these answers is *yes*, it is time you faced the facts: when it comes to taking standardized tests, your child is just like everyone else.

Most Americans experience some fear and nervousness before taking a big test. It is only natural that a child would feel anxious when faced with a test that might cause her to have to take summer school or maybe even be held back a grade. Sure, there are a few folks out there who are perfectly calm when faced with exams, but they are all either hopelessly insane or currently making a living writing test preparation materials.

Let your child know that it is normal to be nervous about the unknown but that the more she knows about the test she is about to take, the less nervous she will feel. All the information and all the techniques we will cover in this book will ease your child's nervousness and replace it with confidence by making that unknown—in this case, the exams—familiar and manageable. Test anxiety almost invariably leads to a lower test score, so it is important you work to boost your child's confidence level. Just understanding the basic format of an exam can be empowering. It can transform a math test from a scary, unknown experience into something as simple as an untimed test with 60 multiple-choice questions worth one point each followed by three to four extended-response questions.

Learning about question types and little details serves a dual purpose: it provides your child with useful information, and it takes away the fear-of-the-unknown aspect of the test. This principal is the foundation of successful test preparation:

Familiarity leads to confidence.

Think of a standardized exam as that haunted house on the end of your street. At first, your child only knows the horror stories about the children who went inside never to be seen again. Your job as a parent is to guide your child through the exams, showing them how the scary noise coming from upstairs is caused by a rusty blind, and beyond the usual dangers associated with an old house (loose floorboards or a rickety staircase), there is nothing about the place to worry about. If you can replace the anxiety and stress your child feels

The End-of-Sentence Game

For a fun way to quiz your child about basic test format facts, try playing this game. For one evening (or longer), try to sneak in simple questions at the end of ordinary sentences so that, "Please pass the potatoes" becomes "Please pass the potatoes if you know how many multiple choice questions there are on your upcoming Science exam." Your child has to answer as quickly as possible and correctly, as well. The game can be played with your child working to get as many right in a row as possible or with asking questions such as, "Dear parental unit, would you please read me a bedtime story and tell me how many different reading comprehension questions are on the English exam?"

about the exam with a feeling of confidence, you will have done your child a great service.

Learning About the Structure of a Test

There are two main ways to find out the format of a test. One is the Internet. Every annual state test is discussed on the website of your state's education department, which are listed at the back of the book. In addition to providing dates for the test, many sites have sample questions or a version of previous tests. Some sites are very good, whereas others are not as forthcoming.

The second method is to talk to your child's teacher. Your child's teacher can tell you when the test is scheduled and can often answer any questions about the test format you might have. Your child's teacher can also answer some other helpful questions you might have, such as:

1. *How much test preparation is going on at school?*

2. *How are these test results going to be used at school?*

3. *Are there any areas we, the parents, should focus on at home with our child?*

Placing a phone call to your child's teacher is probably the best way to contact them, although you can always try the old ambush-at-the-basketball-game routine if you like. Leaving a brief message gives the teacher time to compose a response and get back to you with the answers you want. Writing an email is also an effective method, although not all schools (or teachers) are technologically accessible.

Learning about the format of the test is merely one strategy. There are many others, such as pacing, which will be covered throughout the rest of the chapter.

Why Cosmos Ndeti, Former Boston Marathon Winner, Would Probably Do Well on Many Standardized Tests

Although Mr. Ndeti, a world-class marathon runner, probably has not had as much work with fractions as your child has recently, Ndeti is very skilled in one crucial test-taking area—pacing. Knowing that he is going to run 26 miles, Ndeti picks a nice, consistent speed at which to run and keeps at that pace throughout the entire race. What he *doesn't* do, and what you should not allow your child to do, is spend too much time in any one area or run out of gas before the race is over.

Although many state-standardized tests are untimed, that does not mean your child should spend four hours on every session. At a certain point, taking too much time becomes as harmful as taking too little; frustration mounts, and boredom and fatigue set in. Perseverance is a noble trait, but on a standardized test, spending 30 minutes answering one multiple-choice question is tantamount to standardized test suicide. Your child should stay focused on the task at hand and never get too flustered by any one question. One or two small breaks during each test are fine if your child feels her brain is getting strained. Tell her to put the pencil down, stretch out her hands and arms, take some deep breaths, and then pick up the pencil and finish the test. If she comes to a question she does not understand, tell her to think of this as a guideline:

Spend up to four minutes trying to figure out the question, then, using the techniques taught in this book, take an educated guess and move on.

Perfection is nice, but your child should not expect to get a perfect score on every standardized test. A much better approach is to shoot for a good score, not a perfect score. In fact, many high-stakes tests have only two real scores: pass or fail. To pass, students need to get approximately two-thirds of the questions right, so it is never worth their while to spend 50 minutes on one question that is stumping them, only to be so mentally fatigued that they do poorly on the rest of the exam. Certainly, you don't want to encourage your child to do less than his best, but he must realize that no one question is so important that it is worth getting bogged down on and upset over. There are always some questions that just seem baffling. Throughout the rest of this book, we'll show you how to teach your child to make good guesses, keep his cool, and stay on pace when faced with a stumper.

In addition to telling your child not to get stuck on one question, you can also encourage the "two-pass" approach to test taking. On the first pass through a test, your child should answer only those questions she can handle quickly and easily, skipping over any questions that leave her confused or require a lot of thought. Seeing a bunch of ovals filled in right away often gives students a quick boost of confidence. On the second pass, tell your child to go a little slower, use process of elimination (a technique we'll discuss in a moment) to cross out any incorrect choices, and then take a guess and move on.

The two-pass system is very helpful on tests that have both multiple-choice and open-ended questions. As their name suggests, open-ended questions are questions that have no answer choices. Your child must write the answer in his own words. Some open-ended response questions require only a word or two; these are often called short-answer questions. Other open-ended questions are more like essays, requiring much more writing. Typically, open-ended questions are worth more points, which is why students like to focus on them. However, these questions are usually much harder than simple multiple-choice problems, and they can take up a great deal of time.

> Throughout the book, *open-ended questions* is the term used to describe both the short-answer and extended-response questions together.

The two-pass system allows your child to answer all the multiple-choice questions first before tackling the short-answer and extended-response questions. This is not to say your child should concentrate on the simple questions while blowing off the harder questions. The point is that the open-answer questions are harder and definitely more involved, and you do not want your child getting sucked into one of these to the detriment of the rest of the exam. By saving them for last, your child can answer all the multiple-choice problems, mentally prepare her brain for open-ended question territory (meaning she understands that these questions will be more involved and take more time than the multiple-choice questions), and then tackle them.

For example, consider a reading test with both multiple-choice questions and open-ended problems. After reading a passage, tell your child to answer all the multiple choice questions on the passage first and then answer the open-ended questions. This shouldn't be too hard to do because the open-ended questions are quite often the final questions for any passage. Still, it is important for your child to realize that these two question types primarily test two different skills. The multiple-choice reading questions predominantly test your child's reading comprehension level, whereas the open-ended questions are more like mini-essays testing your child's writing ability. Your child should focus on one skill (and one question type) and then switch to the other skill rather than jumping back and forth between the two.

To help illustrate the importance of pacing, here's a little test-prep fable you might share with your child:

KAPLAN'S TEST-PREP FABLES: THE TALE OF ISHMAEL THE SNAIL

Call him Ishmael the snail. When all the fish signed up for the annual aquarium obstacle course race, no one gave him much of a chance, but Ishmael was confident of his abilities. The starting gun sounded, and all the contestants took off. The goldfish, Ahab, took the lead, but she got caught up on a whale of an obstacle early on. She couldn't figure out how to get around it, and she never finished the race. The two clown loaches were also very fast, but they made too many mistakes. They kept swimming under the hurdles instead of over them, and they skipped some obstacles completely. They wound up being disqualified. The gourami started out at a good clip, but he fell fast asleep around the plastic plant, and Ishmael passed him up. Ishmael ran the entire course at a steady, constant pace, rarely making mistakes, and when the final results were tallied, Ishmael was the winner. As his reward, Ishmael was named king of the aquarium. He now lives in a plastic castle and rules the other fish wisely and fairly.

The Moral: A steady pace wins the race.

Edgar Allan P.O.E.

One of the biggest advantages about taking a multiple-choice test is that you don't always have to know the correct answer choice. Think about it: the answer is already there staring you in the face. If you find all the incorrect answer choices and eliminate them, you will get the question right just the same. The process-of-elimination technique, known as P.O.E. in test-taker's lingo, is one that good test takers use instinctively but that anyone can learn to do with practice. It is especially helpful on any standardized tests that do not have a guessing penalty. You see, on some standardized tests, a fraction of a point is deducted from a student's final score for every question answered incorrectly. This is known as a guessing penalty, and it is meant to discourage random guessing. However, there is no guessing penalty on most tests. A wrong answer simply results in zero credit, not negative credit, so your child has nothing to lose and everything to gain by making good guesses on questions he is having trouble answering. P.O.E. is the key to good guessing.

To demonstrate the effectiveness of this technique, see if your child can answer the following question:

1. How old are the authors of this book?
   A.   4 years old
   B.   29 years old
   C.   35 years old
   D.   126 years old

If this were not a multiple-choice question, your child would have little to no chance of getting the question right. However, as it stands, she should have narrowed down the choices to either B or C, giving her a 50/50 shot of guessing correctly. Because, as we mentioned, there is no penalty for guessing, she should then pick either B or C and move on to the next question.

Use P.O.E. to cross out incorrect answer choices.

Perhaps the hardest part about using P.O.E. is knowing when to use it. In the above question, for example, how would you know that A and D were incorrect? You could say you used common sense, and that would be a valid answer. In many ways, common sense translates to a basic understanding of what the question is asking and therefore what the possible answers could be. Ask your child the question below, and help her use common sense to get a general idea of what the answer will be.

Thomas had $4, but he gave half of his money away to his friend Jeremy for a plastic bucket. Then Thomas gave away half of his remaining money to buy some gum. How much money does Thomas have now?

Before looking at the answer choices, ask your child the following questions:

Could Thomas now have more than $4?

Could Thomas have no money at all?

Could Thomas have $2?

The answer to all these questions is *no*. The last question is probably the toughest. But even if the question is confusing to your child, she could still look at the answer choices and eliminate some incorrect responses.

   A. $4
   B. $2
   C. $1
   D. $0

Why would answer choice A even be there? Test designers offer choices like A to catch the careless student. They know many students often glance at a question, feel unsure of how to work the problem, then just pick a number from the question that appears in the answer choices. Using the P.O.E.—and thinking about what the question is really asking—can help your child avoid these mistakes.

P.O.E. can also be used on English exams as well as math exams. The incorrect choices are generated the same way they are in the above question: Words are taken from the reading passage and placed out of context as an answer choice. Students who remember seeing the words in the passage mistakenly pick them as an answer choice, never questioning whether the answer makes sense. Here's an example of a typical grade 4 reading question:

1. Where did Farmer Ike keep his cows?
    A. In the barn
    B. In a fenced-in pasture
    C. At a fruit stand
    D. In his house

Which of these choices can be eliminated? Hopefully, your child will recognize C and D as unlikely correct answers. Answer C is wrong because stacking cows into pyramids is much harder than stacking apples and oranges, and D is unlikely because no farmer likes to have dinner interrupted by a stampede crashing through the kitchen. Still, these were actual answer choices because the words "fruit stand" and "house" appeared in the reading passage.

On standardized science exams, using common sense and P.O.E. is quite often the best way to approach a question. For instance, on the question below:

Where would it be MOST dangerous to conduct an experiment with electricity?
    A. In a basement
    B. Next to a full bathtub
    C. Near a radio
    D. In the driveway

Your child doesn't have to know any precise scientific facts about electricity; all she has to know is that electricity + water = a SHOCK. There are public service announcements about this fact as well as cautionary tales she may or may not have heard from you ("I remember the time Uncle Wampus melted his hair by taking a car battery into the kiddie swimming pool"). Even if your child didn't know that fact, she could still use P.O.E. on the answer choices. What's dangerous about a driveway or, for that matter, a basement? Hopefully, your child would look at these answer choices and cross them out and then look at B and say, "You know, electricity and water can be trouble. Out of the two choices remaining, I'll pick B."

So far, all of the examples of P.O.E. have dealt with the multiple-choice questions. Whereas P.O.E. is not the best tool to use when writing an essay, it is a technique that can be used for some open-ended questions. Although these open-ended questions are not as amenable to P.O.E. as a multiple-choice question, the fact is that many test problems are multistep questions requiring the student to do more than one piece of work. On questions such as these, P.O.E. is an excellent tool to find the correct answer or at least to do work that deserves partial credit. For example:

Michael reached into his desk and brought out these seven pens.

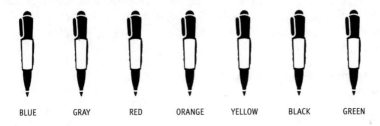

| BLUE | GRAY | RED | ORANGE | YELLOW | BLACK | GREEN |

Michael used one of the pens to color on a map.
Use the clues below to find out which color Michael used.

Clues:

It has less than six letters, but more than three letters in its name.
It is *not* the first or the last crayon.
It is not next to the red crayon.

What color pen did Michael use?

Explain the steps you used to find your answer.

In essence, this question is nothing but a three-step P.O.E. question, although instead of using common sense to eliminate answer choices, you use the clues given to you. With the first clue, you can eliminate red, orange, and yellow. The second clue knocks out blue and green, and the third clue eliminates gray, leaving only black. Even if your child messes up one of the clues and ends up with the wrong final answer, by describing which colors he eliminated and why, he could earn half credit on the question.

Although P.O.E. has many uses, one place where it is not very effective is on the short-answer questions. The short-answer format is specifically designed to prevent test takers from using P.O.E. to find an answer, and in this respect, it is effective. However, there are other ways to skin a cat, so whereas your child cannot use P.O.E on these questions, there are other methods to get the right answer, which will be discussed in later chapters.

Have an Answer for Everything

Suppose your child comes to a multiple-choice math question that she cannot figure out at all. She spends some time looking over the answer choices to see if there are any she feels she can cross out, but nothing comes to mind. P.O.E. fails her. Should she leave this question blank and move on to the next question? The answer is "No, no, no, no, no, a thousand times no!" Again, if there is no guessing penalty, every question should be filled in, even if it means random guessing instead of educated guessing (although educated guessing using P.O.E. is always better, of course). Advise your child to:

1. *Look for ways to work the problem using the appropriate skill . (On the short-answer and extended-response questions, be sure to write down what skill you are applying because discussion of the right technique could earn partial credit).*

2. *Use P.O.E. to cross out incorrect answer choices.*

3. *Guess and move on, knowing that your test grade does not depend on every little question.*

If your son or daughter needs further convincing about the benefits of guessing, you might try telling the following story:

KAPLAN'S TEST-PREP FABLES: THE STORY OF KRONHORST THE FUZZY CHIHUAHUA BUNNY

Early in his life, Kronhorst was just like all the other bunnies. He enjoyed carrots, frolicking in a pasture, and hopping up and down to his heart's content. One day, the Bunny Master came to all the bunnies in the world and said, "OK, it's time you all got ears." (This happened a long time ago, when all bunnies were earless.) The bunnies had several choices: long and floppy, really long and floppy, and tastefully long and floppy, just to name a few. Every bunny made a choice except Kronhorst, who couldn't pick between cute and floppy or trippily floppy.

Not making a choice was the worst thing that ever happened to Kronhorst because from that point on, everyone he met always mistook him for a fuzzy Chihuahua. "Look at that way too hairy Chihuahua!" people would cry, at which point Kronhorst would have to explain that he was a bunny. People would then ask, "But where are your ears?" Needless to say, Kronhorst got pretty tired of these conversations, as well as the endless invitations to the Hair Club's Annual Dog Show... although later in life he did make a lot of money investing in the stock market.

Moral: Answer every question on the exam or people will confuse you for a fuzzy Chihuahua.

Whereas this advice is crucial for the multiple-choice sections, it is no less important on open-ended questions. There might be one open-ended question that looks to your child as if it came directly from the Question Institute of Neptune. If so, tell your child to write *Neptune* next to it and come back later if there is time. However, he must not write *Neptune* more than once on any one session. On all other questions, your child should make his best attempt, and make sure to document his attempt well. Who knows? Your child's guess might be the correct solution, or it might display enough sound math principles to garner partial credit. This is true even on the short-answer questions. Even though your child's chances of answering correctly are very slim if he just guesses randomly, an educated guess has a better chance of being correct than no answer at all.

The Number One and Only Child in the Class

Students are naturally leery of answering a question they do not feel they know the answer to and prefer not to say anything unless they are absolutely sure they are right. Teachers see this all the time in classrooms: children refuse to raise their hands and offer answers to questions because they are afraid of being embarrassed by a wrong answer. Unfortunately, this habit will hurt your child's test score. So explain to your child that on these exams, she should act as if she is the only student in her favorite teacher's class, and if she does not answer, the teacher has to just stand there until she does.

The Only Way to Avoid Mental Mistakes

Your child gains nothing by trying to solve any test problems without writing anything down. Whereas it is impressive if your child can multiply big numbers without using pencil and paper or work out scientific experiments in his head, it's not required for any standardized test. In fact, it even works against his score. Get your child into the habit of writing down all his work on problems and jotting down the main idea of a reading passage as he goes through it. Kids can eliminate a slew of careless errors simply by writing down their work. For many children, writing things down helps them clarify the material. Writing down work during practice sessions also makes for a better learning experience: if your child misses a question, at least you can go back together and see what the problem was.

Write down your work whenever possible.

As stated throughout this chapter, writing down your work is crucial on the open-ended questions. To illustrate this, read the following math example and then see how Imperious Student A and Well-Behaved Student B responded.

Jonathan had $5.00 at the start of the day. At noon, he gave half of his money to Gwendolyn, and at 3:00 P.M. he lost $0.50 in a vending machine.

How much money did Jonathan have at the end of the day? Explain your answer.

Imperious Student A:

Jonathan had two bucks *because I say he did. Now all must bow to the brilliance of Student A!*

Well-Behaved Student B:

Starting out with five, Jonathan gave half, or $2.50, away, so he only had three dollars left. Then he lost 50 cents, so $3.00 - $0.50 = $2.50.

Not only is Student A a megalomaniac, he is also no better than Student B on this short-answer question. Student A provided the right answer with an inadequate solution, earning only partial credit. Student B has the wrong answer but the right explanation, so he gets partial credit as well. Garnering a few points by properly showing your work could significantly boost your child's final score.

Although the example above is math-related, this technique is just as helpful on reading tests as it is on math tests. On the reading passages, have your child take whatever notes she is comfortable with, ranging from writing down the main idea to summarizing each paragraph. You don't want your child to spend a lot of time looking for the perfect phrase to describe the reading selection, but writing down any thoughts she has about the passage will help your child understand the passage better. Because many reading questions are testing just how well your child understands the action in the reading paragraph, any notes your child writes to aid her reading comprehension should lead to an improved score.

"Twas the Night Before the Test..."

Make sure your child feels confident and well rested on the days of the test. Hopefully, this means keeping the nightly routine as regular as possible. You might want to schedule some sort of activity for the nights during the tests, but it should *not* be cramming. Trying to jam in tons of information before a test session is not conducive to a child's test-taking confidence, and it should be avoided.

A positive attitude is more important than any one fact.

If your child does want to review for a while, stick to the basics, asking questions about the test format and general test-taking strategies. These will come in handier than reviewing any particular parts of the different tests. Also, your child will probably answer most of the general test format questions correctly, which will boost her confidence. What you do not want is to have your child stumped by a series of questions because she will go into the exam the next day thinking she is going to do badly.

Here's a handy chart of pointers for the time before an exam.

Things To Do Before and During the Exam

1. Make sure your child gets an adequate amount of rest.

2. Give your child a healthy, adequate breakfast.

3. Let your child have any medication if and only if he takes that medication on a regular basis.

4. Participate in some activity at night that is fun for your child but not too taxing. (Watching a movie on the VCR or playing board games are two ideas.)

5. Give your child positive words of encouragement right before she goes to take the test.

You get the main idea. Send your kid to school relaxed and positive, and don't do anything to upset her normal rhythm. Some things that would *definitely* upset her normal rhythm and as such should be avoided at all costs are included in the following list:

Things Not To Do Before the Exam

1. Send her to bed earlier than usual because she will just have to lie in bed thinking about the test

2. Let your child have any noncritical medication (such as over the counter cold or allergy medicine) that will cause drowsiness or muddled thinking

3. Decide to unwind by watching the midnight tripleheader of Scream I, II, *and* III

4. Decide that the morning of the test is the perfect time to explain to your child how big the national debt really is and what that will mean to her

Review

The main points:

1. Understand the format of the test in question.

2. Maintain a consistent pace throughout the test, and don't let any single question get you flustered.

3. Use P.O.E. whenever possible.

4. Answer every question.

5. Write down all work to avoid foolish mental mistakes and to garner possible partial credit.

6. Make sure you are relaxed and positive on test day.

Questions to ask your child:

1. What 's the moral of "Ishmael the Snail"? *A steady pace wins the race.*

2. What does P.O.E. stand for? *Process of elimination.* Why would you want to use P.O.E.? *Because finding incorrect answers and crossing them out gives you a better chance of answering a question correctly.*

3. What's the moral of "Kronhorst the Fuzzy Chihuahua"? *Answer every question on the test or be mistaken for a Chihuahua with a hair problem.*

4. When should you solve questions in your head? *Never!*

5. Who will love you no matter how you do on these exams? *Your parents, of course!*

Chapter Two READING SKILLS

Getting a Read on Reading Tests

Questions on a fourth grade reading test typically follow a reading passage that is approximately 400 words on average, although it could be as long as 750 words in length. There is usually a mix of nonfiction and fiction passages, although many tests often contain one or two passages in a different format. This different format could be a recipe, website, interview, or some other text that is not as straightforward as a fiction passage. While these passages might seem odd, the strategies needed to solve them are the same as the strategies for nonfiction and fiction passages.

Length for third grade and fifth grade passages will vary slightly. A good rule of thumb on passage length is that 50 words are added for each higher grade level. Therefore, if a typical fiction passage for the fourth grade is approximately 400 words, then a third grade passage averages 350 words, whereas the fifth grade passage would average 450 words. Of course, there are many other factors that effect passage length. Overall, your child should understand that as he advances in grade levels, the length of the typical reading passages advances also.

The number of questions per passage varies but correlates to the length of the passage (the longer a passage is, the more questions after it). Many of the reading passages are culled from existing sources, such as *Cricket* and *Jack and Jill* magazines, which contain amusing, educational, and generally positive stories. If you want to give your child more practice at reading material similar to what will appear on many standardized tests (thus lessening his fear of the unknown), then you should:

Go to a bookstore or library and start reading children's magazines with your child.

This will help on many levels. It will give your child more exposure to reading testlike passages, it should aid in his understanding of such passages (provided you help him with positive guidance), and it should improve his overall reading ability. And, as if that weren't enough, it's also quality time!

The presence of open-ended questions varies from state to state and test to test. Some tests have them, and some do not. For most students, the multiple-choice questions are going to be the problems they feel the most comfortable working on simply because reading a passage and then answering questions is probably something they have done before. Because answering the multiple-choice questions after reading each

> Even when a test does have open-ended questions, multiple-choice questions will still make up the bulk of the scoring. This is another reason why multiple-choice questions should be answered first, because not only are they easier, but they are also what will determine the majority of your child's score.

passage allows your child to work the easier problems first before delving into the more involved questions, this chapter will focus on the multiple-choice questions first before discussing the open-ended problems. If the test your child is studying for doesn't have any open-ended questions, feel free to skip this part of the discussion. In general, multiple-choice questions after a reading passage fall into four major categories:

1. Word Meanings
2. Supporting Ideas
3. Summarization
4. Generalizations and Inferences

Before we can start discussing each question type, we will need a reference passage, such as the sample passage that follows.

Dashiell Learns a Lesson

Dashiell was a happy young ant who was always looking for a way to do things better. Dashiell thought that doing things faster always meant doing things better.

It was summer, and Dashiell and the other ants were busy storing food for the winter. Dashiell would crawl to the nearby field, gather food, and bring the food back to the anthill. It took a long time just to make one trip. Then Dashiell would have to trek[1] all the way back and start again.

"Boing, boing" sounded through the meadow. Dashiell watched as Rebecca Rabbit hopped up next to him.

"Where are you going?" asked Dashiell.

"I'm hopping over to the lettuce patch to get some food," replied Rebecca, who hopped once and then was out of sight.

"Hopping seems better than crawling any day," thought Dashiell. He rose up on his hind legs and tried jumping like Rebecca did but soon fell over on his face. When he looked up, he saw that Aunt Dawn had walked up beside him.

"Rabbits are rabbits," said Aunt Dawn. "You are an ant." Then Aunt Dawn crawled away to gather more food.

Next, Dashiell saw Sylvester Snake pass nearby. "That looks like a good way to travel," he thought. Dashiell laid his body on the ground and tried to slither like the snake did. He twisted his body on the ground for some time but never made any progress. He stopped once his stomach started to get sore. Aunt Dawn saw Dashiell on her way back to her anthill and said, "Snakes are snakes. You are an ant."

Dashiell walked through the meadow. He heard the flutter[2] of wings above his head. Dashiell looked up to see Carol Crow flying around in the air above him.

"What are you doing?" asked Dashiell.

"I'm flying around in search of food," replied Carol Crow, who snatched a tasty grasshopper out of the air.

"Flying seems like the best idea yet," thought Dashiell. He climbed up a nearby rock until he reached the top. Then he jumped off while waving his legs. Dashiell fell to the ground on his face. "Yipes," he cried, rubbing his head. Dashiell looked up and saw Aunt Dawn standing beside him.

"Crows are crows. You are an ant." Aunt Dawn left to get more food and shook her head. "Will Dashiell ever figure it out?" she wondered.

The next morning, Aunt Dawn awoke and saw Dashiell crawling to the anthill with a load of food. "I thought you were going to fly like Carol Crow," said Aunt Dawn.

Dashiell placed the piece of grain down and replied, "Crows are crows. I am an ant."

Aunt Dawn laughed. "I'm glad you learned that lesson, Dashiell. Put that piece of grain away, and then let's go get more food to store in our anthill for winter."

1 walk or travel a long distance
2 flapping

Dashiell Learned His Lesson: Now It's Your Child's Turn

While reading through this passage, your child should be thinking about finding the main idea. What is the whole story about? Having a main idea helps shape the entire story, giving it meaning, which hopefully should help your child in his understanding. However, whereas learning the main idea is important, *memorizing* the main idea is not something your child needs to do. The passage is not going anywhere after your child reads it. It stays right there for easy reference. Teach your child to:

Read to understand, not to memorize.

Once your child understands the action of the story, then it's time to start answering the questions. Children somtimes try to read the story and then answer the questions without looking back into the passage for help. If your child does this, events could get jumbled together, and this will only lead to incorrect answer choices. Tell your child that a standardized reading test is just like an open book test. The passage is there for her to reference, so teach her to feel comfortable going back to the passage to help her answer questions correctly.

LOOKING FOR MAIN IDEAS EVERYWHERE

If your child is unclear on what finding the main idea means, ask him simply to tell you a story about something that happened to him at school today. Because almost every story should have a point, when your child finishes his story, ask him what was the most important thing about what he just said. Another way to phrase this is, "If you had to retell the point of the story again in only one sentence, what would that sentence be?" The most important thing should be the main idea. Looking at a newspaper and discussing how headlines capture the main idea of a news story is another way to talk about the main idea. You can then read the story and come up with your own headlines. One exception: stay away from articles dealing with intricate, high-level finance unless you want your child's head to explode. By the way, if your child likes headlines, you can always play "Night of the Headlines!" where one night everyone speaks only in catchy, single sentences, such as "Child Heads for Bathroom!" or "Argument over TV Remote Leads to Conflict, Then Grounding."

Question Type 1: Word Meanings

Whereas some of the difficult words in a passage often have explanations in footnotes, other words (or phrases) will have questions devoted to them, asking your child, "What does _____ mean?" It is then up to your child to figure out the meaning of the word by looking at the context or how the word is used in the passage. Reading or hearing words in context is actually a good way for

> Word Meaning questions are more common in the third grade than the fifth grade because the emphasis on vocabulary is much stronger at the earlier grades. In later grades, your child will often find more Inference questions, a question type discussed later.

children to learn new vocabulary. It should be stressed that these are supposed to be new words, so your child should not be bothered if the word is foreign to him.

To help your child sharpen his ability to understand words in context, have him focus on the meaning of the entire sentence in which the word appears. Remember, on a multiple-choice test, the answer is already there, so your child just needs a pretty good idea of what the word might mean to tell which answer choices are incorrect or correct. Sometimes the meaning of the unknown word can be gleaned from the sentence it is in, but if the meaning is not there, then either the sentence before or the sentence after will contain the necessary context clues. Your child should never have to look any farther than that: grade school reading tests are just not that rough. As your child looks over these sentences, have him circle any clue words that he feels help him understand the meaning of the word. In other words:

Encircle the underlined word.

After he does this, he should be able to answer a question like the one below.

1. In the story, Dashiell tries to slither like Sylvester Snake. What does *slither* mean?

    A. slide

    B. fly

    C. hop

    D. crawl

Hopefully, your child chose answer choice A. As you can see, Word Meaning questions do not ask students to give the exact dictionary definition of *slither*, just to choose the word or phrase that is synonymous with its meaning. When you ask your child which words led her to that answer, she should say

THE MACKINUTE GAME

A fun way to help your child learn about context is to play the Mackinute Game. Take turns with your child substituting the word *mackinute* into a regular sentence. The other player has to guess what the word *mackinute* means in that sentence. For instance, you might say, "I like my hamburgers with pickles, lettuce, tomato, and plenty of mackinute." If your child answers "ketchup" or "mustard" or some other likely answer, ask her to pick out the words that helped her figure out the definition of the word. Try to make the game as silly as possible. Good luck, and may the best person mackinute!

the words *like the snake did* and the phrase *twisted his body on the ground*.

If your child prefers, tell her to look over the questions before reading each passage and see if there are any Word Meaning questions for that passage. If there are, your child should pay close attention to the italicized word in question when she reads the passage to understand its meaning right away. This may help her feel more empowered about the test, but if it makes her lose track of the overall story line, it's not worth doing. In that case, just have her read the entire story, and then be prepared to go back to where the word is in the passage.

THE MACKINUTE GAME, VERSION 2

In this variation of the Mackinute Game, the rules are the same as before (see "The Mackinute Game"), but the person now has to identify which words acted as clues in the sentence. Therefore, when player 1 says, "I left the *mackinute* in the oven too long and burnt its crust," player 2 now has to say which words (oven and crust) led them to guess that the *mackinute* was a *pie*.

Let's try another:

2. Dashiell rises up on his hind legs in the story. What does *hind* mean?

  A. rear

  B. above

  C. top

  D. front

The sentence with the words *hind* in it contains clues like *raised up on* and *fell over on his face*, which might be enough for your child to figure it out that hind must mean *back* or *rear*. However, the sentence before also contains a clue because Dashiell is discussing *hopping*, an activity that every creature on the planet usually does with its back limbs, whatever they might be.

Question Type 2: Supporting Ideas

Plainly speaking, Supporting Ideas questions test how well students have read and understood small pieces of the passage. These questions are not about the main idea. They are about the little details that, combined, make up the whole of the passage. For example, say you told your child the following story:

A clown in a blue suit walks into a bank with a large duck on his head. The clown goes up to a teller who asks, "Is it hard to keep that thing balanced like that?"

"Not really," replied the duck. "I've got sticky webbed feet."

The Supporting Ideas questions would be things like, "What color suit was the clown wearing?" or "What size was the duck?" These questions ask your child small facts about the passage that he is not likely to remember. If he tries to approach a standardized reading test the way he takes most tests (i.e., by answering questions from memory to test his knowledge), these Supporting Ideas queries are going to trip him up. Therefore, it is important to keep in mind that:

The answers for all Supporting Ideas questions are waiting for you in the passage.

This is another way of saying, "Be sure to look in the passage to answer Supporting Ideas questions." Your child need not trust his memory. Remind him that this is an *open book* test, and using the passage is the best way to get these questions right. From memory, can either you or your child remember which animal Dashiell plays with first? Even if you think you can, it is smart to refer back to the passage to answer this question:

3. Which is the first animal that Dashiell tries to be like?
   - A. Carol Crow
   - B. Aunt Dawn
   - C. Rebecca Rabbit
   - D. Sylvester Snake

Looking back into the passage, your child should be able to pick C or eliminate A, B, and D, leaving C to pick. Either way, it's the correct response.

Knowing where to look takes some understanding of the passage, but with practice, your child should get better at reading a passage for its main idea while keeping a general idea of what events occurred when. Then answering Supporting Ideas questions becomes simply a matter of heading to a particular paragraph, reviewing the information, and answering correctly.

Question Type 3: Summarization

There will undoubtedly be questions throughout the multiple-choice section that ask, "Hey, what's the big idea?" More specifically, these questions want to know "Hey, what's the main idea of this particular story?" Your child can learn to recognize these questions fairly easily because the majority of them are written using phrases such as: "This story is mostly about ____", "What is this story mostly about?" and "What's the main idea of this story?"

Recognizing what kind of question is being asked is very important because the question type determines what strategies your child should use to answer it. In this case, knowing that a particular question is a Summarization question is vital because it means that the answer is *not* stated specifically in the passage. Your child could reread the passage forever and still not find the answer. That's why you should explain that:

To answer the "mostly about" questions, get the Big Picture.

Your child will have to glean a general idea of what the reading passage is about and then use P.O.E. when reviewing the answer choices. Having a general idea of the meaning of the passage helps students separate the right answer from the wrong choices, which is another reason why working on finding the main idea with your child is such a useful activity. The wrong choices are often actual facts from the passage, so they can be very appealing options. But remind your child that just because a piece of information appears in the passage, doesn't make it the *main* idea. A good way to think about it—and if your child can understand this, she's on her way to a successful career as a standardized-test taker—is that wrong answers on Summarization questions are often the right answers on Supporting Ideas questions and vice versa. Get it?

HOW WATCHING TV CAN HELP IMPROVE YOUR CHILD'S SCORE

Granted, there's a catch: it has to be educational television. But if your child enjoys watching nature shows, one way to practice Summarization is to ask your child to summarize sections of these shows in her own words. Nature shows, on channels ranging from *Discovery* to *PBS*, are almost always broken down into segments such as "Here's how the meercats defend their territory," "Two rams fight to see who's the toughest ram in the herd," or "Here a pack of hyenas go to the Automated Teller Machine to get some money for the baseball doubleheader." This game can be played with other shows, but nature shows are a good place to start because the segments often have a general point that is never stated outright by the narrator, who is often spending all his time trying to sound majestic.

Think about the Dashiell passage and what the point of the story was, and then attempt the question below:

5. What is this story mostly about?

    A. Dashiell tried other ways of moving but learned that the ant way works the best for him.

    B. A rabbit, a snake, and a crow all showed Dashiell how they move around the meadow.

    C. Dashiell carried food from the meadow to the anthill and back again.

    D. A crow flew nearby Dashiell, caught a grasshopper, and then flew away.

Whereas B, C, and D are all factual, none of them encapsulates the main point of the story, which is A.

Question Type 4: Inferences and Generalizations

Inference questions, as you might expect, compel the student to infer an answer not stated specifically in the passage. Sometimes the question will have a phrase like *will most likely* in them, showing that the answer is not 100 percent definite, only very likely definite. Like Summarization questions, Inference questions force the student to understand the passage and make deductions from it. For example, after the passage:

Sheryl is sick, but her brother Tommy, who is in grade school, feels fine. Sheryl's three best friends in high school are Angela, Tammy, and Brenda. Brenda lives next door, whereas Angela and Tammy live across town.

An Inference question would be:

> Because Sheryl is sick, who will probably take
> her homework to school for her?
>> A.   Tommy
>>
>> B.   Angela
>>
>> C.   Tammy
>>
>> D.   Brenda

Whereas this example may seem a little arbitrary (What if Tommy's grade school was next door to Sheryl's high school? What if Brenda went to a private school?), the question does contain the phrase *will probably*, which goes to show you that most test writers and DOE (Departments of Education) know the meaning of CYA.

From the Dashiell passage, an Inference question might look like:

6.   Aunt Dawn keeps telling Dashiell "you are an ant" because she:

A.   Wants Dashiell to give up hope of ever improving himself

B.   Wants Dashiell to be comfortable with what he is

C.   Believes that Dashiell should help more with his chores

D.   Is working for the top-secret government shadow agency intent on helping aliens colonize Earth and can only be stopped by two hard-working FBI agents

Nowhere in the passage does it explicitly state Aunt Dawn's reason for constantly telling Dashiell "You are an ant." It is up to your child to deduce from the passage that Aunt Dawn tells Dashiell that because she "wants Dashiell to be comfortable with what he is," or answer B.

P.O.E. can also be used on the above question and not just on answer choice D, the "X-Files trap," which often causes people named Mulder and Scully to perform poorly on this section. It is important for your child to realize that these passages are written at their grade level, and when it comes to emotions:

Good feelings beat bad feelings most of the time.

The reading passages are not written by a bitter, impoverished author angry at the world, no matter what anyone else tells you. They are written by former educators, and because of this, there are no depressing stories about gambling addiction or people fighting and dying in a senseless war. Therefore, if you have an Inference question asking how a teacher feels, you can always cross out answer choices like *angry*, *hateful*, or *moronic*, and if you have a question about why an Aunt Dawn is acting a certain way toward her nephew, you can bet that the reasons are going to be positive ones. Aunt Dawn is not going to believe choice A, which is negative, and C is also borderline stern. The best answer choice is B because it is just the sort of positive, character-building answer that former educators writing the test would want children to learn.

What Kind of Question is *That*?

Knowing the differences between the four question types helps you figure out how to approach each question. To work with your child and help him distinguish all types, discuss the difference between Objectives 1 and 2, which require specific information from the passage, and Objectives 3 and 4, which require your child to interpret information from the passage.

Short-Answer Questions: Get Visual

For the most part, short-answer questions will look like multiple-choice problems without answer choices. Looking at an earlier multiple-choice question:

3. Which is the first animal that Dashiell tries to be like?

   A. Carol Crow

   B. Aunt Dawn

   C. Rebecca Rabbit

   D. Sylvester Snake

The short-answer version of this question would look like:

3. Dashiell tries to act like several different ani-
    mals.
    1) Which is the first animal Dashiell tries to
       be like?

_____

The two questions are essentially the same, only the short-answer question is immune to P.O.E. because there are no answer choices to eliminate.

Like multiple-choice questions, short-answer questions can be answered by referring back to the passage to find the correct information.

Sometimes the process of looking back into the passage takes longer on short-answer questions because students are naturally more cautious when filling in a blank line than they are picking a choice that's already there. This is one reason why short-answer questions should only be attempted after all the multiple-choice questions have been answered: it allows your child to use the two-pass system and work all the simpler problems first.

In addition to having no answer choices present, short-answer can show up in some visual form. An example of this is the wheel-type graphic shown below:

Dashiell tries to act like several different animals. In the circles below, fill in two animals that Dashiell tries to be like.

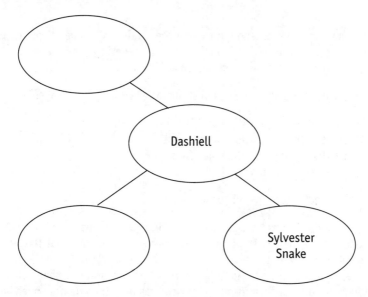

As you can see, the only difference between this short-answer question and the one before it is its appearance. However, if a student didn't know a question like this was coming, they might get flustered by its strange appearance, and getting flustered does no one any good. If you show your child this question and tell him that some of the open-ended questions will have a visual layout, then when he comes to one of these questions, he will have been *expecting* it. Familiarity breeds confidence on standardized tests.

The Extended-Response Questions

The most critical change between multiple-choice questions and the extended-response questions is the one your child is least likely to notice, and that concerns what is being tested. For the most part, the multiple-choice and short-answer questions test how well your child understands a passage, whereas the extended-response questions often test how well your child can write down her thoughts about what she has just read. Both are still tied to the passage, but the added component of writing an answer down in your own words makes it a whole different ballgame.

Make sure your child puts on her writing cap, because putting down a lot of words is one of the keys to performing well on these questions. This is not to say that writing down just anything is effective—your child cannot filibuster her way to a higher score. Instead, being prepared to write down a lot is important because being afraid to write *anything* is a certain recipe for disaster.

Extended-response questions often ask for an answer "in your own words," but your child must back up the answer with information derived from the passage. Therefore, your child must remember:

If you can support your answer with examples from the story, then it is right.

Your child's answer might not be enough to earn the maximum number of points for that question, but if she uses the information from the passage in at least a fairly accurate manner, then she should garner at least partial credit.

Here are two sample extended-response questions on the Dashiell passage.

1. What might have happened to Dashiell if he continued to act like a rabbit for the rest of the year? Use details and examples from the story to explain your answer.

2. Retell Dashiell's story in your own words.

For the first question, your child will have to understand the passage well enough to make some deductions about it. In other words, if your son thought that Dashiell would do just fine emulating a rabbit for the rest of his life, he would not be in a position to gain any credit on this question. However, if your son understands that acting like a rabbit for a long period of time is not going to help Dashiell, then he only needs to write that down and back it up with a fact or or two from the story, such as "Because Dashiell cannot hop like a rabbit, it will be very tough for him to store any food for himself."

At first, your child may be resistant to the extended-response questions because most children prefer to know exactly what the right answer is instead of just jotting down whatever thoughts they have. However, it is crucial to your child's success on these open-ended questions that he feels comfortable putting down his thoughts on paper. If your child is not so thrilled about writing down his own thoughts, here is a story to boost his confidence.

KAPLAN'S TEST-PREP FABLES: THE PRINCESS WHO WANTED TWO BADGERS AND CEMENT BOOTS

Everyone agreed, Princess Lori was without a doubt the most beautiful and difficult person in the entire kingdom. When the king asked whose hand she wanted in marriage, Lori replied she would take the first man who came through the front castle door wearing cement boots and carrying a badger in each hand. From anyone else, this statement would have been called ridiculous, but coming from Lori, it was not even the fourth most difficult request she made that day.

Lured by her beauty, many suitors tried, but all failed. These men learned the hard way that knocking on a door or turning a handle when carrying a badger is an almost impossible task, especially if you have sensitive fingers. And these men were better than most, who got shin splints from wearing cement shoes and never even made it out of the construction area.

But one day, Umbagog the Woodsman came to the castle. A fierce man, Umbagog was so tough that he normally cut down trees just by staring at them until they fell over in fright. Umbagog showed up outside the castle wearing cement shoes with steel girder laces while holding two of the biggest, meanest badgers anyone had ever seen. He took one look at the door and then slammed his head against it, shattering it in one blow. Umbagog then married Princess Lori, and they both lived happily ever after for reasons no one could ever quite explain.

Moral: In tough situations, don't be afraid to use your head.

Another general point your child must remember is that pacing continues to be important while answering extended-response questions. It is very easy to lose track of time when writing an essay. Even on an untimed test, you do not want your child to spend four hours on a single passage. Therefore, tell her to:

Set a pace, and watch your watch.

Of course, this means you will need to give your child a watch to wear (or make sure there is a clock in her classroom) and be certain that she knows how to read it. Whereas proctors will sometimes call out how much time is remaining on the test, it is still up to your child to keep herself on pace. Refer to the chart below for general pacing suggestions:

Question	Time Spent
Reading the passage	5–7 minutes per passage
Multiple-choice questions	1–2 minutes per question
Short-answer questions	2–5 minutes
Extended-response questions	approximately 5–10 minutes, but no more than 15 minutes

Once again, the key is not to spend too much time on any one question at the expense of the entire test.

Chapter Three   WRITING SECTION

Very few states require third graders to write an essay of any kind. This is not the case for fourth and fifth graders, however. By those grades, educators are suddenly very keen to learn how well your child can compose a simple piece of writing. This is why a writing test of some kind usually crops up around the fourth grade.

Some writing tests provide students with a short story and then a prompt statement about it. Although typically, the test your fourth grade child will take consists of a single essay question. If there is a time limit, it is usually around one hour and sometimes a little less. This might seem like a short amount of time, but it is enough to write a tidy, three-paragraph essay.

The essays are graded by teachers according to whatever the grading scale for that particular test is. Although the scale varies from test to test, all essays are graded along the same general guidelines. Teachers review some general writing categories and then decide how well the essay meets the requirements of each category. The following four categories are very typical for a fourth or fifth grade essay:

Category	General Description
Focus	How well does the paper present and maintain a clear theme or idea?
Organization	Is there a coherent structure to the development of the essay, such as a beginning, middle, and end? Are transitional devices used properly? Is there a conclusion?
Support	What is the quality of the details used to support the main idea? Are the details credible, thorough, and elaborate?
Conventions	Does the paper have proper punctuation, spelling, capitalization, and variation in sentence structure?

If your child is tired of studying different facts, equations, and other such information before every test, then the essay test is going to be a breath of fresh air for her. This is because:

All the facts your child needs to write the composition are already in her head.

No more reading passages to refer back to, and no more short essays testing her understanding of a passage. Only one thing is being tested, pure and simple: what kind of an essay writer is your child?

Most fourth grade standardized writing prompts fall into two categories: narrative or expository. Expository prompts ask the students to explain a topic, whereas narrative prompts ask them to relate a story or experience. Therefore, the first thing your child should do when given this exam is:

Figure out whether you are being asked to write an expository or a narrative essay.

It will not help your child's scores on the exam if she writes a detailed explanation about something when the test writers wanted her to write a story. Luckily, it should not be very hard to differentiate between the two essay types because expository prompts often use the word explain, whereas narrative prompts have the phrase tell a story.

Examples of Expository and Narrative Prompts:

Expository: Think of a job you would like to do. Now explain why you would like to do that job. Think of all the places in the world. Now explain why one place is your favorite place.

Narrative: Tell a story about a time when you or someone else found something.

Tell a story about a time you did something that you will always remember.

Here is a sample prompt:

Everyone has done something interesting for the first time. Tell a story about a time when someone you know showed you how to do something for the first time. Or, tell a story about a time when you showed someone how to do something for the first time.

With roughly an hour to write this essay, there is no need for your child to start wildly scribbling down the first idea that comes into his head. Rather, the key to all essay tests can be found in the first 10–15 minutes when your child plans out his response, sketching out an outline of what he wants to say and what details he is going to use to back up his essay. The more specific the details, the better. Look at the sample first sentences below, and see how each one gets more specific and therefore should lead to a clearer, better composition:

This is a story about how I built a car.

This is a story about how I built my first soapbox car.

This is a story about how I built my first soapbox car with the help of my dad.

I remember clearly the day I built my first soapbox car with my father's help: the morning was cold, chilly, as if the night was still battling the sun for possession of the Earth, fighting to keep its spectral, frosty hands wrapped around our fragile planet.

These four examples could be graded poor, adequate, good, and good but a little melodramatic.

After thinking about and planning her essay, your child should spend 20–25 minutes writing. Short, clear sentences are fine. Your child needs to vary sentence structure a bit because graders are looking for varied sentence structure. However, in general, short and simple sentences are preferable to long, complex sentences because the longer a sentence is, the more likely it is to contain a grammatical or punctuation error, which could cost your child points. Remind your child that stylistic brilliance and originality, although both components of excellent writing, are not among the criteria graders will use when reading her essay. She doesn't need to win a Pulitzer here. She just needs to stay focused on a specific topic and express herself clearly and correctly.

After she finishes writing, your child should use any remaining time—and hopefully, she will have 5 or 10 minutes if she stays on schedule—to check her work. One useful proofreading technique is rereading the essay silently-but-out-loud: that is, moving your lips as if you were reading out loud, but not making any noise (because talking is not allowed). This slows students' reading speed down a little and helps them pick up on errors they might otherwise skim over.

If your child can plan, write, and proofread a tidy, three-paragraph essay in 20 minutes, don't force him to use the writing schedule suggested above. There is no need for him to pad an adequate essay, and rambling on until time is up will just muddle the essay and increase the likelihood of spelling, punctuation, and grammatical errors. A speedy writer should use his extra time checking his work.

Chapter Four HOW THE MATH TEST ADDS UP

There are two main question types your child will encounter in a grade school standardized math exam: open-ended and multiple-choice. This is the same as on a standardized English test. As you might expect, because open-ended math problems are harder and more involved, the likelihood of them appearing increases at each higher grade level. Still, some states have standardized tests that are strictly multiple-choice only, regardless of the grade level.

Open-ended math questions are usually harder and more involved, so your child should always:

> **Take the time to answer all the multiple choice questions first, then use any time remaining to answer the extended-response problems.**

If your child is preparing to take a test that has no open-ended questions, tell him to give a silent bit of thanks to whoever made that decision. They can now skip the next section that talks about open-ended questions and go straight to "Calculators, Little Bits of Paper, and Other Stuff."

An Open-Ended Discussion About Open-Ended Questions

Whereas the multiple choice part of the exam is scored by a machine, the open-ended questions are scored primarily by graders (usually teachers) who have been given guidelines about what constitutes a four-point response, a three-point response, a two-point response, and so on. To get full credit, your child has to respond in a manner that is "complete and correct," meaning that not only is the correct answer visible, but there is also adequate work shown that demonstrates how your child arrived at the answer by using her math skills and not her powerful psychic ability. If your child has the correct answer but no explanation, the response is not worth as much. Therefore, as stated earlier, remind your child that on every extended-response question:

> **Show your work, and give every question your best shot using sound math skills.**

The following little fable might help convince your child of the importance of this strategy:

KAPLAN'S TEST-PREP FABLES: THADDEUS THE ARTIST AND THE 51% FIRING SQUAD

One day in the Kingdom of Schmooland, the king's loyal attendants were dusting the king's favorite painting of himself when they made an unwelcome discovery. Some villainous knave had painted a tacky mustache and ridiculous horns on the royal portrait! The whole kingdom went into an uproar, and the king demanded that all subjects search for the person responsible. Eventually, many Schmoolandians started to whisper that Thaddeus the Artist was the person who had made the unflattering additions to the painting. These people had no evidence but were in fact jealous of Thaddeus and his hip, downtown lifestyle that included lots of coffee drinking, black turtlenecks, and incense.

In a rage, the king demanded justice, and although there was no real evidence, a judge declared Thaddeus guilty and ordered him executed.

"But judge," replied Thaddeus, "because there's no actual proof that I committed this crime, isn't it unfair to say that I'm 100% guilty? Isn't it more like I'm 51% guilty, and 49% innocent?" The judge pondered this statement, and realizing that his judgment was only given because the king was angry, decided that Thaddeus was indeed only 51% guilty.

The day of the execution arrived, and Thaddeus was placed before the firing squad. When asked if he had a final request, Thaddeus said, "Because I am only 51% guilty, I should only be 51% executed." The officer in charge of the firing squad agreed and ordered his men to use only 51% of the usual gunpowder. When fired, the weakened bullets bounced off the artist's stiff smock, which was covered in dried paint and shellac. The officer in charge decided he had done his job and let Thaddeus go.

A free man, Thaddeus then proceeded to find the real culprit, and then he wrote a screenplay about his exploits, which was made into a movie starring Harrison Ford that did tremendously well at the box office.

Moral: Partial credit can make a big difference.
Moral #2: Harrison Ford is a big-time box office draw.

All this talk about partial credit is not meant to encourage your child to not worry about getting the right answer. She should not answer the question "What is 7 minus 2?" with the response, "Something around 3." The whole purpose of the discussion is to make sure your child does not freeze up when she encounters a difficult looking extended-response question.

Calculators, Little Bits of Paper, and Other Stuff

Your child may be armed with more than just a No. 2 pencil for some state and national math tests. Many states allow the use of a simple calculator during some or all of their exams. Other states provide students with even more, giving them geometric paper shapes and 6″ rulers that they can use on some questions on the test.

Calculators can help your child avoid mental math mistakes, but they really are not as helpful as you might instantly think. Tests that allow calculators take that into consideration, so your child will never encounter a question as straightforward as:

1. $\dfrac{48}{6} = ?$

    A.   6

    B.   8

    C.   48

    D. 288

Instead, your child will be faced with:

2. There are 48 people who need to be seated at 6 different tables. Each table must have the same number of people seated there. Which number sentence could be used to find out how many people will be seated at each table?

    A. $\dfrac{48}{6} =$

    B. $\dfrac{48}{8} =$

    C. $48 \times 6 =$

    D. $48 \times 8 =$

If it was an extended-response question, the same question might be seen as this:

3. There are 48 people who need to be seated at a restaurant. The restaurant has 6 different tables. Each table must have the same number of people seated there.

    A. How many people are seated at each table?

    B. In the space below, draw a diagram to represent this information.

    C. If the restaurant found two more tables in the storeroom and used them as well, how would this affect the number of people at each table?

    D. Two-thirds of all the guests leave by 10:00, and

the remaining guests gather together. How many
tables do the remaining guests need to use?

All three questions pose the same math problem, but to answer questions two and three correctly, the student must be able to say to himself, "Hey, this is a division question." (The third question, as you may have noticed, was an extended-response problem.) Having a calculator might be helpful for question 3, but it doesn't really help on question 2, does it?

In the end, your child should consider calculators, rulers, little paper shapes, or any other stuff she receives as tools that could be useful during the exam. They provide her with options that she might need to answer some questions on a test. This is good because the more ways you can approach a question, the better your chances of getting to the right answer are. Although overall, whereas a calculator might be helpful, the most important tool still lies between her two ears.

What the Math Test Tests

There are many different ways to name and categorize basic grade school math skills. For example, many states like to combine strands 3 and 4 into a single category, Geometry and Measurement.

No matter how you slice them, the basic math skills remain fairly constant nationwide. Geometry and Measurement questions are the same from test to test, regardless of whether or not they are in one category or two. The only way they would be different is if one state considered a four-sided figure a square while another called it a triangle. Then this country would have problems and not just on standardized tests.

Luckily, a square is a square and a fraction is a fraction no matter where you are. The following content strands cover the basic grade school math concepts, and the rest of this chapter will discuss them in detail:

CONTENT STRAND:

Strand 1: Number and Number Relations

Strand 2: Algebra

Strand 3: Measurement

Strand 4: Geometry

Strand 5: Data Analysis and Probability

Strand 6: Patterns, Relations, and Functions

These questions test a student's knowledge and understanding of such basic math principles as whole numbers, integers, even/odd numbers, consecutive order, decimals, fractions, ratios, percents, and irrational numbers (all the basics you learned as a child but have long since forgotten). What makes these concepts difficult is how they are presented on the test. Some of the questions are very straightforward, such as:

Number and Number Relations questions are found throughout the third to fifth grade. However, harder concepts, such as fractions and ratios, will not be featured as much in the third grade. Generally, your child will encounter simpler problems concerning even-odd numbers (like the piggy bank problem) in the third grade. Harder concepts will appear in the fourth and fifth grade level.

70 quarters   15 quarters   33 quarters   25 quarters

Which of these piggy banks has an even number of quarters?

A. 70 quarters

B. 5 quarters

C. 33 quarters

D. 25 quarters

Unless your child makes a careless error, chances are good she will get A as an answer. Other problems, however, are not so obvious.

The students at Piedmont Elementary are collecting sticks for an art project. The pictures below show the number of sticks they have collected so far.

Sticks Collected
Week 1

Sticks Collected
Week 2

Sticks Collected
Week 3

How many sticks do the students have after collecting them for three weeks?

A. 808

B. 880

C. 708

D. 826

This is a question that covers up what it is asking fairly well. The trick is for your child not to get flustered if he does not understand what to do initially. He should ask himself, "What does this question want me to do with all these numbers?" After some calm thought, he would probably realize the answer is, "Add them together."

Make sure your child is comfortable with basic math terms.

Some of the more popular terms to know are fractions, ratios, and percents. Your child can be fairly certain there will be a question or two on each of these topics, so it is important that she truly understands and feels comfortable with these subjects. A question involving these terms might look like this:

4. Evelyn has twelve donuts. One-fourth are glazed, one-third are chocolate, and the rest are plain. What fraction of the donuts are plain?

    A. $\dfrac{1}{4}$

    B. $\dfrac{1}{3}$

    C. $\dfrac{5}{12}$

    D. $\dfrac{7}{12}$

On a question like the one above, just being able to recognize a fraction will not be enough to get this question right. A clear understanding of how fractions work is needed. On the question above, three of the donuts should be glazed, and four are chocolate, leaving five plain. The answer would then be $\dfrac{5}{12}$, or choice C. You could have also used P.O.E. to eliminate A and B, since both those fractions appeared in the question itself.

Petty Bribery

To help your child work with fractions and other basic terms more, simply add these types of questions to the Bribery Game. With percents, you should start with a dollar, since 100 cents = 1 dollar, so the number of cents is always the percentage of a dollar (25 cents = 25%). Gather like groups of currency together to work on fractions. For example, you might use a group of eight dimes and ask your child "If I had $\dfrac{1}{4}$ of these dimes, how many cents would I have?" For ratios, using two different groups of change would work, such as gathering six dimes and two nickels and asking, "What is the ratio of dimes to nickels?"

Here is an extended-response Number and Number Relations problem:

1. Prakash and his father were playing a game where one person would think of a number, and the other person would have to guess the number from certain clues. The first clue Prakash gave was, "I am thinking of a three-digit whole number that has the digits 2, 9, and 5."

    A. List all the numbers that Prakash could be thinking of.

    Prakash's next clue was, "This number is also a multiple of 5."

    B. List all the numbers that Prakash could be thinking of now.

    Prakash's last clue was, "When my number is rounded to the nearest hundred, it is 300."

    C. What is Prakash's number?

    D. Write three clues for another number game and number your clues.

The game must have only one correct answer. Write the answer.

Quite a question, eh? This shows again why it's best to leave the extended-response questions to the end. Prakash's second clue, "This number is also a multiple of 5," basically asks your child to decide which of 259, 295, 529, 592, 925, and 952 can be divided by 5. Once again, it's a division question, of sorts, but it doesn't come right out and announce itself.

Your child would have to do a bit of work to answer part D. Whether or not he cares to spend his time in this endeavor is entirely up to him, but the key point is: it should be done last.

Strand 2: Algebra

This strand covers basic Algebra, so your child will not have to fret about long strings of variables. Also, many states do not emphasize Algebra in grade school, so whereas your child will probably have at least one to two questions on the subject, it is unlikely to be a major math category. (The major math strands are Number Sense, Geometry, and Measurement.) A typical algebra question appears below:

What number does q stand for in the equation below?

$$(7 + 3) + 5 = 7 + (q + 5)$$

A. 3

B. 5

C. 7

D. 12

Caution is the name of the game on this question. Your child can do the math, and so long as she writes down all her work and does not make a careless error, she should get the right answer. Or, she could look at the question and see that because only addition is involved, the numbers on both sides of the equation have to be the same. Because the right side of the equation is missing a 3, $q = 3$. Either way, the answer is A.

Strand 3: Measurement

These questions test your child's knowledge of such measurements as length, width, area, volume, time, temperature, and angles. In other words, does your child know how to find a perimeter as well as the area of a rectangle? Can she determine which questions ask her to find the perimeter and which questions ask about area? She might encounter a question like this:

> It helps if your child is comfortable with all the various area, perimeter, and volume formulas for the most basic shapes before taking the test. However, this is not always necessary because many standardized tests provide a list of common formulas at the front or back of their math test. Be sure to find out whether or not this is the case on the test your child is preparing to take.

A group of construction workers stacked bricks in the shape below. Each brick measures one unit on each side. What is the volume in cubic units of this stack of bricks?

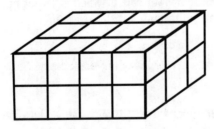

A. 8 cubic units

B. 12 cubic units

C. 18 cubic units

D. 24 cubic units

There are two solutions to this problem. The first requires your child to remember that volume = length × width × height, and so the numbers 2, 4, and 3 will need to be multiplied together to get 24. The other way would be for your child to look at the illustration and use common sense. Eight bricks are showing, but there are definitely more than eight, so answer choice A can be crossed out. At this point, it is either guessing time or your child could now put together 8 x 3 (because it is three rows deep) and get 24.

Another kind of Measurement problem centers on questions such as, "Does your dog weigh 15 kilograms or 15 meters?" These Measurement problems test whether or not your child understands the basic units of measurement, and because no one uses metric units (but everyone knows they should), you can expect that these problems will usually test metric terms.

Jimmy the Wonder Slug, shown below, was found recently on a South Pacific island. The picture shows the actual size of the slug. Which of the answer choices below best describes the length of the slug?

A.   5 kilometers

B.   5 meters

C.   5 centimeters

D.   5 millimeters

If your child picks A, then he has probably had nightmares of monstrous slugs destroying whole cities in their slime trail. The correct unit of measurement is C, centimeters.

Strand 4: Geometry

Whereas Measurement questions dealt with geometric formulas concerning area, width, and so forth, Geometry questions test students in several different categories.

Category	Example
1. Knowledge of different geometric shapes	How is a cylinder different from a cone?
2. Knowledge of geometric terms	What is symmetry? What is congruence?
3. Understand how an object will look	What will Figure X look like if flipped upside down?

To tackle Geometry questions:

Know all your basic two- and three-dimensional figures.

Two Dimensional	Three Dimensional
Triangle	Pyramid (with triangular or rectangular base)
Square	Cube
Circle	Sphere
Rectangle	Cylinder
	Cone

Knowing these figures is the critical first step to answering Geometry questions well. Knowing these definitions backwards and forwards is even better.

ACTiViTY: SUGAR CUBE CASTLE

For a time-intensive but fun way to teach your child about two- and three-dimensional shapes, buy a box or two of sugar cubes, get some glue, and construct a small castle using the cubes. All the basic shapes should be used: the towers could be cylinders, the front wall a rectangle composed of cubes, and pyramids and triangles can be placed along the tower wall. To make a sphere, some careful nibbling will have to be done, but who doesn't like sugar?

Which of the figures shown below is a rectangle?

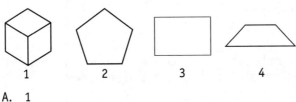

A. 1

B. 2

C. 3

D. 4

If your child knows her shapes, the answer C is fairly simple. If she doesn't know her shapes, then it's back to the sugar cubes for ye!

In addition to shapes, Geometry questions ask about such geometric terms as congruence, symmetry, similarity, and reflections. Again, questions will generally not be as straightforward as, "What is the definition of congruency?" Instead, the question would give a figure, such as a rectangle, and then ask, "Which of the following figures below is congruent to rectangle ABCD?" The student would then have to pick a congruent rectangle from among the answer choices. The correct answer will probably be "disguised" in some way, like being rotated 90 degrees.

Another type of Geometry question places an emphasis on spatial sense. Students get a nice, geometrical figure to start with, such as:

and are then asked to pick this figure out of a lineup after it has been spun, turned, or rotated in some way. For example:

Which of the figures below shows the top figure after it has been flipped both vertically and horizontally?

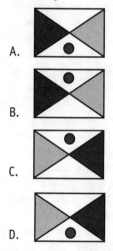

A.

B.

C.

D.

Two basic test-taking techniques come into play on a question like this. First, there is P.O.E., allowing your child to at least eliminate figure D because it is the original figure. The second important strategy is to show your work. Do not have your child doing these mental flips in her head—have her draw the figure flipped horizontally, and have her flip the figure vertically. Artistic brilliance is not necessary, and neither is an ability to figure out this question in her head. Your child should sketch out the two flips, which should not take too long. Even if it does take three minutes, three minutes spent getting a question right is better than spending two minutes getting a question wrong.

Strand 5: Data Analysis and Probability

The Data Analysis part of strand D consists of two types of questions involving graphs and charts: simple and advanced.

> Simple = your child must read the graph correctly.
>
> Intermediate = your child must read the graph correctly and do some sort of mathematical computation.
>
> Advanced = your child must make the graph correctly.

The simple and intermediate graph questions are multiple-choice problems. Your child will encounter the simple problems in third grade, and the intermediate problems will appear in grades four and five. The advanced questions are extended-response questions that your child could encounter as early as the fourth grade, but it would be highly unlikely to see anything like that on a third grade standardized test.

Graph problems may feature multiple questions referring to the same graph, and they look like this:

The graph below shows how many raffle tickets Ms. Diaz's class sold during one week. Study the graph, and then answer the following questions:

ACTIVITY: FOR THOSE OF YOU SCORING AT HOME

Various kinds of charts are scattered throughout every newspaper, but if you want to go to the place that charts call home, turn to the scoreboard page of the sports section. There you will always find as many charts as there were games last night. Explain to your child what the various markings mean, and then ask questions such as "Who had the most hits in this baseball game? or "How many more runs did the Astros score in the fourth inning than the Mets?" Questions like "This bum playing shortstop went hitless and yet still got paid $400,000 for the game. Where's the justice in that?" are socially relevant, but should not be asked to your child because they very rarely appear on standardized tests.

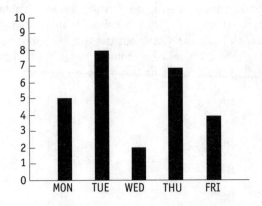

Ms. Diaz promised the class could work on their art project on the day the total number of tickets sold reached 16. The bar graph shows the number of tickets sold each day.

(Simple question)
On what day did the students sell eight raffle tickets?

A. Friday

B. Thursday

C. Wednesday

D. Tuesday

(Intermediate question)
How many days did the students sell more than six tickets?

A. 2

B. 3

C. 4

D. 5

The first question requires that your child read the graph correctly. That's all. Looking at the number 8 and then moving across, you can see that the answer is D, Tuesday. For the intermediate problem, your child needs to read the graph and then use the information in some manner. The second question is essentially a P.O.E. question: Which days can be eliminated because fewer than six tickets were sold? Only two days are left, leaving answer A.

An extended-response question might look like this:

Ms. Diaz's class sold raffle tickets for one week in order to pay for an upcoming class trip. The results are shown below.

On the grid below, make a bar graph showing the number of raffle tickets sold each day. Use the information on the table above to help you.

Be sure to:
- title the graph
- label the axes
- use appropriate and consistent scales
- graph all the data

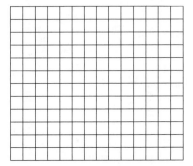

Using the information from your graph, write two statements comparing ticket sales on the lines below.

_____

_____

At this point, no doubt many of you are feeling grateful that you do not have to take this test. Granted, this is an extended-response question and deservedly so, but it can still be completed if your child feels good about making charts. Any number of answers to the second part could be correct. Graders want your child to show that he can interpret the graph he just created. A correct answer could be a statement like: "There are only two days where the students sold more than 6 tickets. The students reached 16 total tickets on Thursday."

In addition to charts and graphs, some questions will deal with probability. (This is not likely to happen in the third grade, although it is a remote possibility.) These questions can come

CHART YOUR VEGETABLES!

To give your child some experience making charts, you first need to buy some grid paper. Then, it's just a quick trip into your kitchen, where you can ask your child to graph all sorts of items. How many vegetables are there? How many different types of soups are there? Make sure that your child always puts numbers along the vertical line and a description of what is being graphed along the horizontal line. The rest is counting. If your child does a thorough job of graphing your food supplies, be sure to use the information on your next shopping trip. While everyone else has a shopping list, you will have a shopping grid.

in many different forms, so there is not really any one particular question setup your child should be on the lookout for. Luckily, there will probably not be very many of these questions on the exam. Don't spend too much time trying to explain the concept to your child. You may frustrate and worry her unnecessarily. If she is curious, you can try using a die to explain the general principal. Show her that there are six total sides on the die, each with a different number of dots. The probability that any side will appear when you roll the die is one in six. That's the basic idea. It is probably best to leave the discussion at that, unless you want to confuse yourself and your child.

Strand 6: Patterns, Relations, and Functions

"Prepare for launch: 6, 5, 4, 3, 2..."

What number comes next? If your child knows the answer to that question, she is on the path to answering Pattern questions. Problems in this category can either be visual patterns or a mathematical pattern involving a set of numbers. A simple pattern question will look like this:

Study the pattern below.

What is the next shape in the pattern?

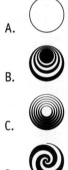

A.

B.

C.

D.

On questions like these, tell your child to be prepared for patterns in groups of three or four, like the problem above. Why these two numbers? Whereas it would be rash to say that there will always be three to four shapes that repeat, consider what the test-designers' thought process must have been. They probably thought a pattern involving groups of two would be too easy. Five is a remote possibility, but that would be very difficult, so three or four are the prime suspects every time. Because it is a four-character pattern above, the answer is A.

On questions involving repeating patterns, first look for patterns that repeat after every three to four characters.

Questions that ask you to add up the parts that make up the pattern are a little tougher, and they often look like the problem below:

This staircase is four steps high.

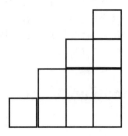

What would be the total number of squares if the staircase were six steps high?

A. 10

B. 15

C. 21

D. 24

To solve this type of pattern problem, just continue the pattern, and then add things up. There are 10 squares to start with, so adding 5 squares and then 6 more would make 10 + 5 + 6 = 21. Then it's off to the answer choices! Our old friend P.O.E. could help if your child got stumped on this pattern question. Clearly, if we started with 10 squares and then added more steps, choice A could not be correct. Your child can cross out this choice and then take a guess.

Whew! Believe it or not, that's all the math. It may seem like there is a lot for your child to remember. There is. But practice using the activities suggested in this chapter (and any others you can think of), and she will be up to speed in no time.

Chapter Five I GOT A WHAT?!

How to Interpret Your Child's Test Scores

Your child's scores will be broken down into three main categories: a scaled score, an achievement level score, and a percentage subscore.

On annual state standardized tests, the achievement score runs along the lines of: excellent, good, passable, needs improvement, and failing. These are the major categories your child's score will be placed into. Depending on the state you live in, a failing score could mean your child would have to repeat the grade or do something to improve his or her score.

The scaled scores are a more precise breakdown of the achievement level scores. For example, consider a state that uses a scaled score from 200–500. The minimum scaled score needed to receive a good rating in this state is 300. Therefore, a child who scores 310 and a child who scores a 320 will both receive this ranking, but the second child's test score was better than the first child's score. The scaled scores are used by some states to create precise rankings of how every school did when compared with other schools.

Internet Information

Instead of achievement levels, many nationally used standardized tests use a scale of 0–99 to show results. This number is supposed to illustrate how well your child did in a hypothetical national classroom of 100 students. If your child scores a 63, that means she did better than 63 other students, giving her a hypothetical rank of student #64. On this scale, a highest score would be 99 because all other 99 students did not do as well on the exam.

In addition to the scaled score and the achievement level, your child will also receive a percentage score in the Math, Reading, and other content categories. The Math content categories are the ones discussed at length throughout the book: Number and Number Relations, Geometry, Measurement, and so forth. The percentage subscores show how well your child performed on all those types of questions, so if she receives a 75% on the Geometry subscore, then she answered three-fourths of all those questions correctly.

Whereas a low score can be a cause for concern, it should not necessarily be considered an indication that your child is lagging far behind in his studies and that his education so far has been worthless. Be sure to discuss his scores with the person who is very knowledgeable about your child's ability as a student: his teacher. Your child's teacher will provide a better, more complete overview of your child's academic standing than a single score from one standardized test.

It is important that parents keep these scores in perspective. Every test should be seen for what it is: an interesting checkpoint along a very long highway. Some students who scored at the lowest level on a certain test will go on to graduate from prestigious universities with advanced degrees, whereas other students who scored at the top will struggle to finish high school. Your child's scores simply highlight where your child needs improvement, and the best person available to make sure your child receives that improvement is currently reading the last sentence of this book.

RESOURCES

List Of STATE EXAMS, GRADES 3-5

The following list is provided to give you an idea of what tests are required in your state. This information is always changing. Please contact your state's department of education or your child's school if you need to make certain that these requirements are current.

State	Test Name	Grades
Alabama	Alabama Direct Assessment of Writing (ADAW)	5
	Stanford Achievement Test, Tenth Edition (Stanford 10)	3–5
Alaska	Alaska Benchmark Exam (ABE)	3–5
	TerraNova Cat – Complete Battery Plus	4–5
	Standard Based Assesments (SBA)	3–5
Arizona	Arizona's Instrument to Measure Standards (AIMS)	3,5
	Stanford Achievement Test, Ninth Edition (Stanford 9)	3–5
Arkansas	Arkansas Benchmark Exams (ABE)	4
	Stanford Achievement Test, Ninth Edition (Stanford 9)	5
	Iowa Test of Basic Skills (ITBS)	3–5
California	Standardized Testing and Reporting (STAR)	3–5
Colorado	Colorado State Assessment Program (CSAP)	3–5
Connecticut	Connecticut Mastery Test (CMT)	4
	Direct Reading Assessment (DRA)	3

State	Test Name	Grades
Delaware	Delaware Student Testing Program (DSTP)	3–5
District of Columbia	Stanford Achievement Test, Ninth Edition (Stanford 9)	3–5
Florida	Florida Comprehensive Assessment Test (FCAT)	3–5
Georgia	Criterion-Referenced Competency Tests (CRCT)	3–5
	Iowa Test of Basic Skills	3–5
	Grade Writing Assessment	3–5
Hawaii	Hawaii Content and Performance Standards, Second Edition (HCPS II)	
	Stanford Achievement Test, Ninth Edition (Stanford 9)	3,5
Idaho	Idaho Reading Indicator (IRI)	3
	Idaho Standards Achievement Test (ISAT)	3–5
	Direct Mathematics Assessment (DMA)	4
	Direct Writing Assessment (DWA)	4
Illinois	Illinois Standards Achievement Test (ISAT)	3–5
Indiana	Indiana Statewide Testing for Educational Progress (ISTEP+)	3
Iowa	Iowa does not have a statewide testing program, but the majority of districts there use the Iowa Test of Basic Skills (ITBS)	3–5
Kansas	Kansas Assessments	3–5
Kentucky	TerraNova	3
	Kentucky Core Content Tests (KCCT)	4–5

State	Test Name	Grades
Louisiana	Iowa Test of Basic Skills (ITBS)	3,5
	Louisiana Educational Assessment Program for the 21st Century (LEAP 21)	4
	NAEP 2005 will be administered to a sample of students in 2005	4
Maine	Maine Educational Assessment (MEA)	4
Maryland	Maryland School Assessments (MSA)	3,5
Massachusetts	Massachusetts Comprehensive Assessment System (MCAS)	3–5
Michigan	Michigan Educational Assessment Program (MEAP)	4–5
Minnesota	Minnesota Comprehensive Assessments (MCA)	3,5
Mississippi	Mississippi Curriculum Test (MCT)	3–5
	Mississippi Science Test is being developed	5
	TerraNova	4
Missouri	Missouri Assessment Program (MAP)	3–5
Montana	Iowa Test of Basic Skills (ITBS)	4
Nebraska	Nebraska does not currently have a statewide testing program. Districts may choose either the California Achievement Test (CAT), the Iowa Test of Basic Skills (ITBS), the Metropolitan Achievement Test (MAT), Stanford Achievement Test, Ninth Edition (Stanford 9), or the TerraNova.	4
Nevada	Nevada CRT	3,5
	Nevada Writing Assessment (NWA)	4
	TerraNova	4

State	Test Name	Grades
New Hampshire	New Hampshire Educational Improvement Assessment Program (NHEIAP)	3
	New England Common Assessment Program (NECAP)	3–5
New Jersey	New Jersey Assessment of Skills and Knowledge (NJ ASK)	3,4
New Mexico	New Mexico Achievement Assessment Program (NMAAP)	3–5
	New Mexico Writing Assessment (NMWA)	5
New York	New York State Testing Program (NYSTP)	3–5
North Carolina	End of Grade (EOG)	3–5
	Science assesssments will be added in 2008	5
	NAEP sample testing	4
North Dakota	California Achievement Test (CAT)	4
	North Dakota Reading Test	4
	North Dakota Writing Test	4
Ohio	Reading Achievement Test	3–5
	Writing Achievement Test	4
	Math Achievement Test	3–5
Oklahoma	Oklahoma School Testing Program (OSTP)	3–5
Oregon	Oregon Statewide Assessments (OSA)	3,5
Pennsylvania	Pennsylvania System of School Assessment (PSSA)	5
Rhode Island	New Standards Reference Exam (NSRE)	4
	Rhode Island Writing Assessment (RIWA)	3
	Rhode Island Health Education Assessment	5
	NAEP	4

State	Test Name	Grades
South Carolina	Palmetto Achievement Challenge Tests (PACT)	3–5
	NAEP	4
South Dakota	State Test of Education Progress (STEP)	3–5
Tennessee	Tennessee Comprehensive Assessment Program (TCAP)	3–5
Texas	Texas Assessment of Knowledge and Skills (TAKS)	3–5
Utah	Core CRTs	3–5
	Reading Diagnostic Test	3–5
	NAEP	4
	Iowa Test of Basic Skills (ITBS)	3,5
Vermont	New Standards Reference Exam (NSRE)	4
	VT-PASS	5
	New England Common Assessment Program (NECAP)	3–5
	Writing Portfolio	5
Virginia	Standards of Learning (SOL)	3,5
	Stanford Achievement Test, Ninth Edition (Stanford 9)	4
Washington	Iowa Tests of Basic Skills (ITBS)	3
	Washington Assessment of Student Learning (WASL)	4,5
West Virginia	Stanford Achievement Test, Ninth Edition (Stanford 9)	3–5
	West Virginia Writng Assessment	4
Wisconsin	Wisconsin Knowledge and Concepts Examination (WKCE)	4
	Wisconsin Reading Comprehension Test (WRCT)	3
Wyoming	Wyoming Comprehensive Assessment System (WyCAS)	4

List Of STATE TEST WEBSITES

The following list is provided to give you an idea of where you may find out more. This information is always changing. Please contact your state's department of education or your child's school if you need to make certain that these websites are current.

State	State Education Department Website
Alabama	http://www.alsde.edu/html/
Alaska	http://www.educ.state.ak.us/
Arizona	http://www.ade.state.az.us/
Arkansas	http://www.arkedu.state.ar.us/
California	http://www.cde.ca.gov
Colorado	http://www.cde.state.co.us/index_home.htm
Connecticut	http://www.state.ct.us/sde/
Delaware	http://www.doe.state.de.us/
District of Columbia	http://www.k12.dc.us/dcps/home.html
Florida	http://www.firn.edu/doe/doehome.htm
Georgia	http://www.doe.k12.ga.us/
Hawaii	http://doe.k12.hi.us/
Idaho	http://www.sde.state.id.us/Dept/

State	State Education Department Website
Illinois	http://www.isbe.state.il.us/
Indiana	http://ideanet.doe.state.in.us/
Iowa	http://www.state.ia.us/educate/index.html
Kansas	http://www.ksbe.state.ks.us/Welcome.html
Kentucky	http://www.kde.state.ky.us/
Louisiana	http://www.doe.state.la.us/
Maine	http://www.state.me.us/education/homepage.htm
Maryland	http://www.msde.state.md.us/
Massachusetts	http://www.doe.mass.edu/
Michigan	http://www.mde.state.mi.us/
Minnesota	http://cfl.state.mn.us/
Mississippi	http://www.mde.k12.ms.us/
Missouri	http://services.dese.state.mo.us/
Montana	http://www.bpe.state.mt.us/
Nebraska	http://www.nde.state.ne.us/

State	State Education Department Website
Nevada	http://www.nde.state.nv.us/
New Hampshire	http://www.ed.state.nh.us/
New Jersey	http://www.state.nj.us/education/
New Mexico	http://sde.state.nm.us/
New York	http://www.nysed.gov/
North Carolina	http://www.dpi.state.nc.us/
North Dakota	http://www.dpi.state.nd.us/
Ohio	http://www.ode.state.oh.us/
Oklahoma	http://www.sde.state.ok.us/
Oregon	http://www.ode.state.or.us/
Pennsylvania	http://www.pde.psu.edu/
Rhode Island	http://www.ridoe.net/
South Carolina	http://www.sde.state.sc.us/
South Dakota	http://www.state.sd.us/deca/
Tennessee	http://www.state.tn.us/education/

State	State Education Department Website
Texas	http://www.tea.state.tx.us/
Utah	http://www.usoe.k12.ut.us/
Vermont	http://www.state.vt.us/educ/
Virginia	http://www.pen.k12.va.us/
Washington	http://www.k12.wa.us/
West Virginia	http://wvde.state.wv.us/boe/
Wisconsin	http://www.dpi.state.wi.us/
Wyoming	http://www.k12.wy.us/wdehome.html

GLOSSARY

Assessment: Measurement of student achievement at a specific point in time. It can be compared to a snapshot that captures a single moment in a student's academic career. Any type of task that a teacher uses to measure student knowledge or ability, from a multiple-choice test to an essay or project, qualifies as an assessment. You will want to find out from your child's teachers what kinds of assessments they use, how often they use them, how they align with the content standards (see below) for the course, and whether or not they help prepare the student for standardized state tests.

Authentic Assessment: Any assessment that involves students in *real world* activities. Assessments can be termed *authentic* if they approximate adult work activity (managing money, applying for a fictional job, etc.) or if they immerse students in real-life situations (composing letters to the newspaper editor on current issues). Because many of the new state tests use *authentic tasks*, you may want to ask what the student's coursework is doing to help him or her prepare to do such tasks and what you can do to support your child at home.

Benchmark: Standard by which something can be measured or judged. In education, benchmarks are samples of student work that set a standard by which other students' work can be judged. Referring to benchmarks gives both students and parents the opportunity to examine work that has met the standard; they show what an excellent product looks like. When you meet with your child's teachers, ask if the course has a set of benchmarks to examine and how the teachers use them in instruction.

Content Standard: Statement of what students should know and be able to do at the end of a course. It indicates what students should learn and what kind of learning activities the teacher needs to provide. Content standards usually head the curriculum description; therefore, all the learning activities of the course should help students to meet those standards. You are entitled to see the curriculum for each course your child takes and should feel free to ask questions about how the teacher accomplishes the content standards through daily class work.

Criterion-Referenced Test (CRT): A test that specifies a particular goal for students to achieve. A criterion-referenced test lists the characteristics of student work that demonstrate mastery. That list should be available to students and parents to help them understand what the task demands. When you discuss standardized tests with a teacher, you may need to ask which tests are criterion-referenced.

Evaluation: Analysis of student achievement over a period of time. The term is often used interchangeably with assessment, but it more specifically refers to long-term student work, such as a portfolio of art or writing or a project that demands that the student use an entire semester's worth of learning to complete.

High-Stakes Test: Any assessment with real consequences, in the form of rewards, sanctions, or intervention, attached to performance. Often, the outcome of a high-stakes test determines whether or not the student will be promoted to the next grade or graduate (see exit exam). In some states, the *stakes* in question vary. Students who perform well, for example, may receive special recognition or monetary rewards; those performing poorly may be remanded to summer school. Schools and school districts are not immune to the consequences of high-stakes tests either because the results of such tests are often used to determine the amount of funding that school receives. You should inquire as to the consequences, if any, of your state's assessment.

Holistic Scoring: A technique that is more concerned with the whole than with analysis or separation into parts. Readers of essays and other written tests who score holistically assign a score based on their impression of the work as a whole. In contrast, traditional assessment of writing usually analyzes parts, such as outline, thesis, organization, spelling, etc. In standardized tests, holistic scoring is done by a minimum of two readers who receive training in the criteria for scoring. This is done to ensure consistency and fairness. It is important to ask which assessments are scored holistically.

Norm-Referenced Test (NRT): A test that compares an individual's score to the scores of a group of individuals. Test makers analyze the scores of a representative reference group who took the test beforehand and determine percentiles of achievement. Therefore, students' achievements are being compared to the achievements of the students in that reference group. Norm-referenced assessments like the SAT and the ACT have raised controversy in the past when questions surfaced about how representative their reference groups are. NRTs such as the Stanford 9 and ITBS are also known as "off-the-shelf" tests.

Performance Assessment: Task that requires a student to demonstrate what he or she knows and is able to do. There is some similarity to an authentic assessment, but students may be asked to demonstrate knowledge strictly related to the academic content of a course without necessarily engaging in real-world activities. Teachers are often very proud of the performance assessments they have created and are happy to display them when they meet with parents. You will want to look at them in the context of the content standards to see if they are in alignment.

Performance Standard: Statement that describes the individual tasks a student performs to demonstrate that he or she has met the content standards. Good performance standards give clear descriptions of what the teacher expects and show students how to meet those expectations. They should be published well in advance of the task so that students and parents can ask questions to clarify their understanding of what is expected.

Reliability: Consistency of test scores. A test that is reliable will produce consistent results. Students who take two different forms of the same test given in the same year should get similar scores on both forms. The test maker must provide documentation to the school that the test is reliable.

Rubric: A set of concise descriptors used for assessing student work, often organized in a grid to provide descriptors for four to six levels of achievement. Rubrics exist in many forms, but all give very specific descriptions of what student work should look like. Good rubrics help educators be more specific in assessing student work. They should be available to students in advance of doing a performance task so that they understand what is expected of them and how to meet those expectations. A good question to ask teachers is whether they use rubrics, how often, and whether they give them to students with enough advance notice to be helpful in completing the task.

Validity: Assurance that a test actually measures what it is supposed to measure. For example, if a test is supposed to measure students' knowledge of basic French grammar, it is invalid if it uses advanced vocabulary. Just as with reliability, test makers must document the validity of the test.

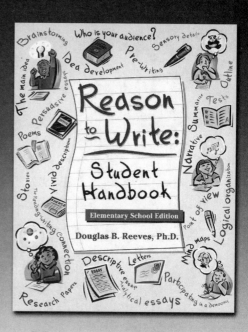

Get Ready for an
Adventure!

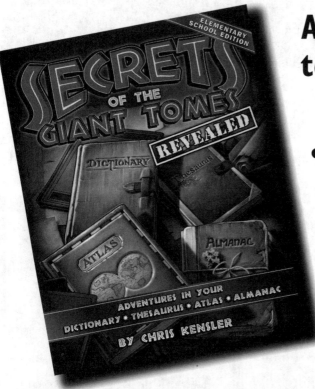

Activities that teach children how to use:

- **a dictionary**
- **a thesaurus**
- **an almanac**
- **an atlas**

Tennessee Toledo, *a daring young explorer, guides your child through these important reference books as he attempts to uncover the greatest archaeological discovery of all time!*

Also by Chris Kensler:
Secret Treasures and Magical Measures: Adventures in Measuring

Published by Simon & Schuster